C000199997

*An exploration of three typefaces
using traces found in Venice,
Bologna and on a tin of tomatoes.
Each font is reconstructed as a
forensic anthropologist would build
an identity from a solitary bone.*

3 FOUND FONTS

AN EXPLORATION

Jake Wilson

Jake Wilson

TRE CARATTARI TRICOLORE

Gabriella Bassano

The three typefaces explored in this book all vary in their degree of foundness. As Roland Barthes said: texts are *'a tissue of quotations drawn from the innumerable centres of culture.'* A similar system of quotation and reinvention exists when designing a typeface. One of Jake Tilson's aims in creating *3 Found Fonts* was to examine their origins, context and influence on their surroundings. He researched, reconstructed and extended each typeface. An architectural methodology assisted this process by utilising typographical precedents as a guide and to suggest a solution for missing characters. When using precedents ideas of design authorship and copyright are explored. A font's family tree is often convoluted. Tracing origins requires careful detective work, particularly in a world obsessed with ownership, tracibility and a shrinking public domain. In an article written for the *'Collaboration and Ownership in the Digital Economy'* conference, the sound artist Joe Banks cites a

model of 'good practice' in relation to intellectual copyright found in the science-research community, *'the requirement for the open, accurate attribution of the sources from which the ideas, data and arguments used in research are drawn.'* {1}

Banks' phrase *'open referencing of sources'* describes part of the impetus that led Tilson to produce this book and CDROM. The line between being a plagiarist and a researcher can be thin, fortunately a documentary air of tangential preservation prevails in

3 Found Fonts. The juxtaposition of seemingly random elements extends the narrative content, resulting in a vortex of ideas and source material that openly reveals his sources and thought processes.

To emphasise this position he repositions the fonts back in the world as *Open Source* software, even supplying the *Fontographer* files he used to create the fonts for others to use. By supplying the code without licence he diffuses the notion of singular authorship. As with Tilson's

Gabriella Bassano is one of the founders of the Istituto di Carattere in Siena.

previous work a collage aesthetic permeates the process through appropriation, manipulation and finally distribution for use by others.

Working with fonts that come with baggage he opens the bags, shows us some of the contents and hides a few items of his own before shutting it and passing it on.

§ A TIN OF TOMATOES §

The display font *Pomodori* is imagined from finding only six characters on a tin of Italian tomatoes in the Tuscan hill town of *Cortona*. *Pomodori's* decorative arabesques become strangely contemporary as Tilson grapples with the additional two hundred and fifty characters he designs in order to form a complete typeface. A distant collaboration occurs between the original, unknown designer of the six characters and Tilsons' extension of the font. The underlying structure appears modular, derived perhaps from an early, brushed design or an 1800's woodblock typeface. The tangential research into its' possible origins take him to North America in the 1800's and to luxury food packaging whose logotypes retain an essence of their woodblock ancestry. His desire to turn the *Pomodori* characters into individual rubber-stamps neatly brings the life cycle of the font back to its Gutenberg roots – that of an inked impression on paper. He hopes other designers might develop additional weights of the font from his source code.

§ BOLOGNA §

I met Tilson several times in Bologna to discuss the project. We always ate at *Tamburini*, a *Bistro Self Lunch* restaurant/deli in the gastronomic *via Caprarie*. The second font in his Italian trilogy uses the smudged, minuscule typography found on a *Tamburini* cash register receipt for its starting point. It was a serif font, which he found unusual. A contradiction in itself as a vertically stressed serif font that is bitmapped, monospaced and thermal. However, he felt it suited the setting and location. The receipt contained thirty-three characters so his job of recreation would be more straightforward than with the tin of tomatoes. By rounding what would have been a squared matrix from the thermal cash register the final font retains a used feel, particularly in smaller sizes.

§ CALLI, CAMPIELLI E CANALI §

Tilson's third Italian typeface strays from a culinary source, moving onto the street. Of his three fonts this has the most documentary feel and is identifiable as being of Italian origin. Designer-artists are obsessed with the typography that surrounds them as I found out when walking the *Calli e Campielli* of Venice with him. His font, *Nizioleto*, takes its name from the whitewashed rectangles in which Venetian place names are stencilled. With the aid of a marked-up map of Venice indicating rarely used characters, such as **W**, he sets out to photograph the available alphabet. As with the *Tamburini* font he produces a typeface that reveals the facture of its usage. The letterforms reflect process and handling as the ragged nature of the stencilled characters on stuccoed walls is celebrated. To extend this used appearance he has produced a variation set of characters that are accessed by using the lowercase keyboard.

The found quality in each font is expressed in different ways from the cross-referenced, extended approach in *Pomodori*, the thermal simulation of *Tamburini*, and the ragged, Venetian edges of *Nizioleto*. But to label these fonts as merely found does his work on them a disservice. As a consummate collagist with an eye for detail on the lookout for difference, his exploration of these chosen fonts extends beyond the visual appearance of their characters. I myself now look away from the centre screen action in films starring James Stewart, on the lookout for bifurcating fonts in street signage.

Tilson recently had two CDs of his photographs chosen for *FontShop Internationals' fstop* photo library. *Public Toilets* and *Urban Noir*, black and white photographs, mainly of New York. *3 Found Fonts* adds to this redistribution of his source material for use by others.

{1} **Joe Banks** > The Case of Authors, designers, Engravers, Etchers, Film Makers, Musicians, Photographers, Scientists, Scupltors, Conceptual and Sound Artists &c, 2002.
http://proboscic.org/diffusion/

Also see > General Notes on the Preparation of Scientific Papers, Royal Society, 1974.

POMODORI

A B C D E F G H I
J K L M N O P Q R
S T U V W X Y Z

A decorative, digital, revival typeface designed from only six existing characters found on a tin of tomatoes in Cortona, Italy.

TYPE SPECIMEN PAGES > The character set for this font includes: uppercase, lowercase, numerals and accented variants for most Latin script languages.

Ä Å Ô Á Ã Â Ç Ð
É È Ë Ê Í Ì Ï Ñ Ö Õ
Ó Ô Ò Û Ú Û Ù Ü Ÿ

£ € $ ¢ ₣
₽ ! % ® ©

£ € $ ¢ ₣
₽ ! % ® ©

% = < + > /

. , : ; b ¡ ... · " "

' ' ¿ « » < > ( )

( ) ( ) ¯ ° ™ .

gate 54

0 1
2 3
4 5
6 7
8 9

a b c d e f g h i
j k l m n o p q r
s t u v w x y z

á â â ä ã å ç @ é
è ê ë í ì î ñ ó ò ô
õ ú ù û ü ü á à ẞ

KEYWORDS ›
tuscan, bifurcating, revival, decorative,
display, 1800's american, wildwest,
letterpress, poster, woodblock,
gastronomic.

§ A TIN OF TOMATOES §

Food packaging is a fertile outpost for uncharted fonts, old logos and antiquated print finishes. Five minutes from my studio in Peckham are some of the most ethnically diverse independent grocery shops in London. Their shelves of produce put me in touch with the output of graphic designers from every continent, and in the dustier corners you can step back through the century. A non-brand supermarket is a good place to be - difference rather than homogeneity. Shopping abroad in markets and supermarkets helps ground me to the location as I check out packaging and produce. I know a war correspondent who visits a barber in each port of call to adjust to the local rhythm of the city, for me a heaving bag of groceries to a kitchen and cooking a meal has the same effect.

Stepping down into a green grocers in Cortona, Italy, I saw a beautiful tin of tomatoes. I bought the tin for its typography alone. Back in London I wrote, e-mailed and faxed the producers outside Naples trying to glean information about their trademark and logo. After a web search I wrote to the other seventy-eight processed tomato producers in Italy asking for sample packaging. Eight replied. I then attended a symposium titled *'Is Copyright a Good Thing?'* at the *Institute of Contemporary Arts*. A complex issue with conflicting advice for artists and type designers. The visual appearance of a typeface design seems not to be copyrightable, whereas the fonts name (trademark) and the software to distribute it (font suitcase) is copyrightable. Elsewhere I found conflicting data. On the CD I will supply links to specific websites so you can make up your own mind.

§ A, I, L, M, O, P §

The underlying structure of the six, found uppercase characters made the re-design of certain missing letters straightforward. However, drawing the lowercase and numerals was problematic, requiring a tall x-height due to thick serifs. To assist the blind recreation of what was missing I hunted down other bifurcating fonts - where each serif splits in two. Looking at the relationship between uppercase and lowercase fonts and their various stems, descenders, bowls, ears and spurs helped me to define a visual approach and set some rules. An early attempt with the lowercase using an equal count of serifs as the uppercase fell apart when tested on a sample sentence or two. Beautiful but illegible. Tuscan bifurcating typefaces were popular in Victorian Europe and used for North American 1800's woodblock type. They were also an accomplice in Hollywoods' re-branding of the wild west {1}. During this project I produced a visual identity for a Cumbrian lamb farmer {**www.whitbysteads.co.uk**} for whom I researched gastronomic labelling and packaging in upmarket London food halls and farmers markets. This search netted many bifurcating fonts and logos that may have developed from a woodblock lineage. Victorian shop and pub fascias still preserve handcrafted examples. I spent days online surrounded by typography books. I asked friends at *FontShop* to help identify the typeface. The closest we all came was ***Wyoming Macroni*** by Robert Schenk. But it's not close. If anyone finds a match please email me {**jake@thecooker.com**}

{1} Idea courtesy Robert Schenk

Pomilia
Italian peeled tomatoes.
Wrap-around paper label.
Found in Cortona, Italy

OTHER BIFURCATING FONTS
Fonts with double-ended stems

Maille
Sherry vinegar, France.
Found in Tesco, Inverurie,
Scotland

Ferrero
Company logo, cacao box.
Found in Supermercato Punto,
Dorsoduro, Venice

Coniglio
Fresh rabbit, paper label.
Found in Coop, Camucia, Italy

Bonifanti
Logo from a panettone box.
Found in East Dulwich Deli,
London

Chatka
Tinned crab pate, Kamchatka,
Russia. Found in Fortnum &
Mason, London

Wardour
Company logo.
Smoked oysters box.
Found in Peckham, London

Vegetable display
Via Nazionale
(was Via di Ruga Piana)
Cortona, Italy

MAILLE

Vinaigre de
XERES
Importé d'Espagne
SHERRY
Vinegar
Imported from Spain

MAILLE

Vinaigre de
XERES
Importé d'Espagne
SHERRY
Vinegar
Imported from Spain

£3.49   £2.49   MAILLE SHERRY VINEGAR 500ML

FERRERO

BONIFANTI

WARDOUR
FAMOUS FOODS

Maizena
Maize flour
Found in Supermercato Punto,
Dorsoduro, Venice

MAIZENA®

A M I D O *di* M A I S

PER DOLCI SOFFICI E LEGGERI

ollitura della frutta

apec

eparare
fette

Zabar's delicatessen
Carrier bag
New York City

KENNEDY

J. KENNEDY L^{TD}

Alex Kennedy Ltd
Meat products factory and shop,
Peckham, London

Kam Foh Chinese Takeaway
Restaurant facia
Peckham Road, London

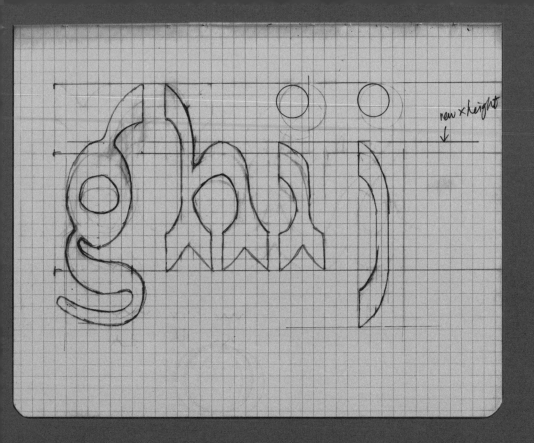

new x height

Sketchbook - Jake Tilson
Lowercase g,h,i,j
London, 2003

Film - **Rear Window**
Director - Alfred Hitchcock, 1954
Starring James Stewart
Art direction - Joseph MacMillian Johnson and Hal Pereira

Film - **Winchester '73**
Director - Anthony Mann, 1950
Starring James Stewart

TAMBURINI

TAMBURINI

A B C D E F G H I
J K L M N O P Q R
S T U V U W X Y Z

Inspired by thirty-three characters found on a cash register receipt in the shop/bistro Tamburini in Bologna, Italy.

Ä Å Â À Ã Á Ç D
É Ê Ë È Í Ï Ì Ñ Ö Õ
Ó Ô Ò Ù Ú Û Û Ù Ü Ÿ

£ $ ¢ ? ! & °
% ® © @ €
£ $ ¢ ? ! & °
% ® © @ €

‰ = < ☧ > / ° ∴ ¡ ¿
… " " ' ' , « » ‹ ›
( ) [ ] ⟨ ⟩ / | \ * ™ –
_ – – ∨ ÷ ≈ × ˘ ° °

653@Art

0 1
2 3
4 5
6 7
8 9

a b c d e f g h i
j k l m n o p q r
s t u v w x y z

á à â ä ã å ç é
è ê ë í ì î ñ ó ò
ô ö õ ú ù û ü fi fl

E ?

KEYWORDS >
serif, bitmapped, thermal, Italian,
sampled, gastronomic, bistro.

§ VELICIBO' §

Go through to the back room, it overlooks the heat of the street and is flooded with natural light. Sit by the left at the door. This side entrance to the bistro needs to be pushed hard to open, *SPINGERE*, creating chances for chatting to passers by. Beggars with cards and cans sneak in through the side door where staff can't anticipate their entrance. *Tamburini* is positioned at the heart of a world class gastronomic square mile in Bologna, in Emilia-Romagna, Italy. Founded in 1932, *Tamburini* sells only hand made produce. The shop brims over with it. Pork produce is made from animals slaughtered only in winter. Fortunately for visitors lacking a nearby kitchen to cook in there is a self-service restaurant to taste much of their produce. Stacked chestnut and oak firewood rests near the wood fired oven as a queue forms quickly at noon with dusty builders, white-collar workers and the occasional foreigner. Check with your local customs department before buying ham to take home, otherwise buy fresh *tortellini*, *piadina*, an unsalted Tuscan loaf and a bottle of *Sangiovese Tamburini*.

> *"One of the best food stores you will ever set foot in."*
>
> Fred Plotkin
> *Italy for the Gourmet Traveller*.

> *"When you hear mention of Bologna's cuisine, make a bow, for it deserves such respect."*
>
> Artusi

§ TORTELLINI IN BRODO §

Fresh tortellini requires only a simple recipe. In Bologna a favourite method is to cook the tortellini in stock, making a light soup. The hot, thin soup provides a perfect support to unlock the taste of each individual tortellini, keeping them warm until you eat the last one. A bag of fresh tortellini will keep in your fridge for a few days or can be frozen. It is traditionally eaten on Christmas Eve in Bologna.

You will need: One pint of light chicken or fish stock, thinned slightly with water. A quarter kilo of fresh tortellini, or less. Parmesan cheese and unsalted Tuscan white bread.

Bring the stock to a rolling boil, add the tortellini and some salt if your stock was unsalted. Simmer for about five minutes or until the tortellini rises to the surface. Ladle the broth and cooked tortellini into wide shallow bowls. Add a little freshly grated parmesan. Serve with a slice of lightly toasted unsalted Tuscan bread, rubbed with a clove of garlic. Add a little salt and olive oil. In Tuscany bread is often placed in the bowl before soup is poured over it.
Serves 5

This book's CDROM has other *Bologna* restaurant recommendations.

Bologna city map
Jake Tilson
Collection
Virmelskirchen Kunstverein

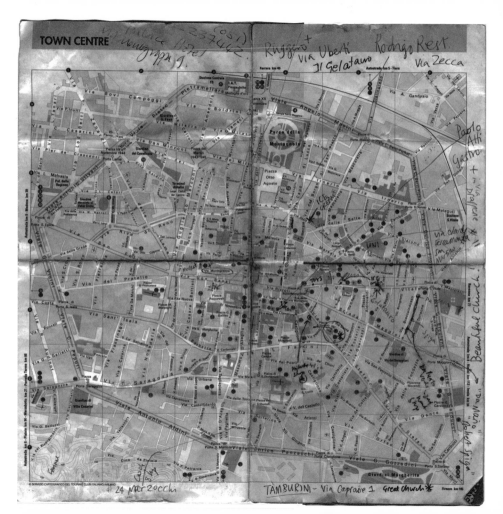

TOWN CENTRE

Handwritten annotations around the map:

via Palace (Sre) ~Z37422 (os1)

Umagrappa 1

Ringgero +   Via Uberti   Rodrigo Rest.

Il Gelataio   Autostrada/km 5 - Fiera   Via Zecca

Via A. Gandusio

Paolo Atti
Gastro

via Clara Ferramonta
con Alistina

Beautiful church! →

TOYS

24 Marzocchi

TAMBURINI - Via Caprarie 1   Great church ✱

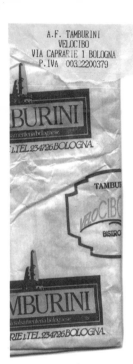

SANGIOVESE

GNOCCHI ALL'ORTICA FRESCHI

PIADINE DI RICCIONE

MORTADELLA

REP.PASTA 12,37
A.F.TAMBURINI S.R.L. 23952

VIA CAPRARIE N.1 BOLOGNA

| Rep. 1 | | Bilancia 5 | # 013156 |
| 17.07.2002 10:57:09 | | 411/5 | Oper. 3 |

kg	Tara kg	€/kg	€
0,514		16,53	8,50

Impostazione manuale

3,87

2 Voce Somma €

17 LUG 2002

RTELLINI
RINI FRESCHI
€
al KG. 23,24

Primi piatti   Rigatoni al pasticcio
Crepes ai carciofi   Rigatoni alle melanzane
Garganelli ai carciofi   Rigatoni speck e...
Gnocchetti   Rigatoni al prosciutto e cipolla
funghi   Risotto ai gamberi e vongole
Maccheroncini alle verdure   Risotto peperoni
Mezze penne al pesto   pesto genovese
Nidi di rondine al forno   speck e radicchio
Penne ai carciofi   Tagliatelle alla cipolla dolce
Penne al... gorgonzola e noci   Cannelloni
Pennette alla zingara   palombo al forno
Pennette alle vongole e gamberi   carciofi

Arista agli asparagi
Arista al **Portafoglio alla bolognese**
Arista con prosci**Prosciutto al forno**
Arista speck e **Prosciutto al Soave**
Arrosti mist**Rollè di vitello al forno**
Carni alla g**Scaloppine al limone alla**
Costata di v**pizzaiola, agli asparagi**
Fesa**Spezzatino di vitello con piselli**
File**Spiedini e insalatina mista al forno**
Filetto al limon**Straccetti alla rucola**
Involtini di ca**Tacchino ai pomodorini**
Lombo allo**Tranci di palombo al forno**

Pollo allo spiedo

NIZIOLETO

NIZIOLETO

ABCDEFGHI
JKLMNOPQR
STUVWXYZ

A digital, revival typeface based on the stencilled street names of Venice.

Ä Å Â À Ã Á Ç
D É Ê Ë È Í Ï Ì
Ñ Ö Õ Ó Ó Ò
Ú Û Ù Ü Y ® ©

£ € $ ₡
& ? ! %

£ € $ ₡
& ? ! %

\# % ‰ § = < + >
/ ´ ` , :; ¡ ¿ … . '
" ` ´ " « » ‹ › ( )
| { } / | \ * ™
· ~ ˆ O × ¨ ¯ ≠ ª
≤ ≥ × ≈ " " I ˇ ˜
@

RAGU 56

0 1 2 3 4
5 6 7 8 9

0 1
2 3
4 5
6 7
8 9

NUMERI CIVICI > The numerals above use the **civic building number** character set.
SUPERMERCATO GARIBALDI > A second set of numbers (right) uses a supermarket window display stencil as its source.

KEYWORDS >
tuscan, bifurcating, revival, decorative, display, 1800's American, wildwest, letterpress, poster, woodblock, gastronomic.

In Venice a house numbering system existed before streets were named. A number was given to every building in the two main zones of *de ultra* and *de citra* creating two vast progressive series of numbers. These are called *Numeri Civici*. During the second Austrian Dominion of Venice in 1841 the system changed. Each of the six *sestieri* (boroughs) had their own progressive series of building numbers. They still exist today such as **Cannaregio 1** through to **Cannaregio 6368**. From the late XII century, the government of the Serenissima had proposed a new toponomy and some time between 1834 and 1841 with the publication of the new *Avviso*, for place names, a form was fixed. These white washed rectangles on which place names are stencilled are called *nizioleto/nizioleti* in Venetian, translated from the Italian *piccolo lenzuolo/a* – little

1 PRINCIPAL WATERWAY
CANAL GRANDE

2 ZONES	
DE ULTRA	DE CITRA
OUTSIDE	INSIDE

6 SESTIERI	
DISTRICTS	
SANTA CROCE	CASTELLO
DORSODURO	CANNAREGIO
SAN POLO	SAN MARCO

38 PARISHES · 100 ISLANDS
127 SQUARES · 177 CANALS · 354 BRIDGES

sheet, bed sheet, small sheet. The size and typeface were set as *roman*. A few recent street names appear as stone-carved *nizioleti* such as **Campo S. Fantin** and **Ponte de la Guera**, but they are rare. So are the occasional hand lettered *nizioleto* such as **Calle del Dose Da Ponte**. Today, after a building has been re-stuccoed, the job of re-stencilling the place name is

carried out by the *Comune di Venezia*, although the work may fall to subcontractors. Further research is needed to pinpoint the introduction of stencilling as opposed to hand lettering. It is tempting to attribute the typeface used to Giambattista Bodoni (1740-1813) whose **Bodoni** (1798) provides many distinctive characteristics found in the nizioleti font – such as the curved

Bodoni Titling Bitstream

MQREA

Bauer Bodoni Adobe

MQREA

Bauer Bodoni Bitstream

MQREA

Nizioleto Atlas

MQREA

Didot

MQREA

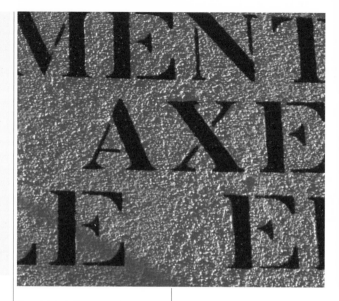

leg of the **R**, **E** and the parallel, vertical stems of the **M** and the general straightened up nature of the font. However the character width seems too wide for pure *Bodoni* and the use of bracketed serifs on the **A** where one might expect a line serif are problematic. Further peculiarities such as the tail of the **Q** dissecting the bowl is unusual in Roman fonts – although I found both versions in

the nizioleti. I assume there are different stencil sets being used causing this variation. The origin of the typeface therefore seems to stem from stone carved lettering and shop-sign painting traditions as opposed to that of a traceable series of typefaces designed for printing on paper by Bodoni, Didot or Fournier.

Non dissecting Q
Ramo Quarto Rio Terà
Castello

Dissecting Q
Campiello del Squero
Castello

New and old stencil sets?
Rio Terà Canal
Dorsoduro

Stuccoed walls
Calle de la Verona
San Marco

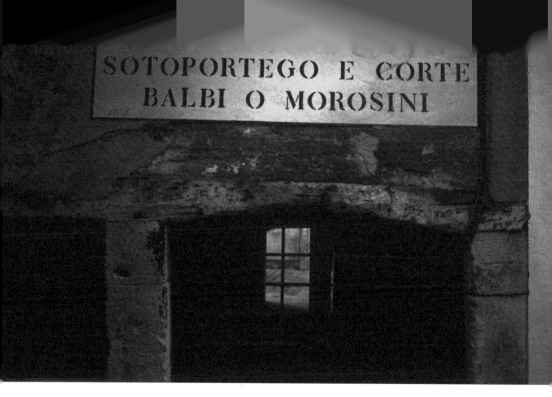

Sotoportego e corte Balbi o Morosini
Castello
Sotoportego - a street running under a house. Corte - courtyard

Riva S. Biasio - Sestier de Castelo
An alternative spelling of Castello

Ramo Quarto Rio Terà
Castello
Rio Terà - a filled in canal

Calle del Forno
Forno - oven

Campiello Caboto
Campiello - a small campo without a church

Parochia S.Francesco da Paula
Parochia - parish

Salizada Malipiero
Salizzada - one of the first paved streets

Polenta con le seppie
In Venetian, **Poenta e sepe**
Polenta and squid
Trattoria All 'Antico Pizzo
Rialto, San Polo, 814

NUMERI CIVICI

0 1 2 3 4 5 6 7 8 9

SUPERMERCATO GARIBALDI

Supermercato Garibaldi
Via Garibaldi
Castello

Rialto market, San Polo
Campo de la Pescaria -
looking across at the Palazzo
Michiel 'dalle Colonne' rebuilt
in 17th C. on a pre-existing
Gothic building

FLAVIA MORTON TRUST

PUBLISHED BY
Atlas
16 Talford Road London SE15 5NY
info@areaatlas.com
www.areaatlas.com

DESIGN
Jake Tilson & Associates
jake@thecooker.com
www.thecooker.com

PRINTING
Furnival Press, Atlas Factory
and Smith Kellett

BINDING
Muir, London

PAPER
Monadnock Dulcet 100lb
alkaline pH, acid-free,
from New Hampshire, USA

CD DUPLICATION
10th Planet, London

TRANSLATION
Bucatini, Rome

FONTS
Typeset in Interstate designed by
Tobias Frere-Jones, Caslon Old Face
from Bitstream, and Nizioleto,
Pomodori and Tamburini designed
by Jake Tilson.

SUPPORTED BY
The New Geography Federation grants
to artists scheme and The Flavia
Morton Trust.

COPYRIGHT
©Jake Tilson 2003

ISBN
ISBN 0 907508 37 5

DISTRIBUTION
art data - tel 44 (0)20 8747 1061
orders@artdata.co.uk

WITH THANKS TO
Jennifer Lee, Hannah Tilson, Joe & Jos
Tilson, Anna and Sophy, Sara Fanelli,
David Blamey, Stephen Kirk, Pieter May,
Gary Baker, Michael Marriott, Gabriella
Cardazzo, Paolo Cardazzo, Fiona
MacLeod, Gill Scott, Sue Hunter, Johnny
Gumb and Keith Herbert at Furnival
Press, FontShop International, Gabriella
Bassano, Damien Poulain, Studio
Architetto Maurizio Rosa, Joachim
Ackersohn, Robert Schenk, The New
Geography Federation.

BOOK
This book was published to coincide
with Ways of Saying, a Loman Street
Studio project, commissioned by
Stephen Kirk, curated by David Blamey
featuring: Michael Marriott, Jake Tilson
and David Blamey, London - 2003.